THE
Spiritual Traditions of
SEX

RICHARD CRAZE

THE
Spiritual Traditions of
SEX

*A unique look at sex
as a spiritual experience*

RICHARD CRAZE

*Harmony Books
New York*

For Jen Tieh Fou who showed me the Tao

Published by Harmony Books, a division of Crown Publishers, Inc., 201 East 50th Street, New York, New York 10022. Member of Crown Publishing Group.

Random House, Inc., New York, Toronto, London, Sydney, Auckland.

HARMONY and colophon are trademarks of Crown Publishers, Inc.

Originally published in Great Britain by GODSFIELD PRESS in 1996

DESIGNED AND PRODUCED BY
THE BRIDGEWATER BOOK COMPANY LTD

Printed and bound in Hong Kong

Library of Congress Cataloging-in-Publication Data

Available upon request

ISBN 0-517-70566-4

10 9 8 7 6 5 4 3 2 1

First American Edition

The publishers wish to thank the following for the use of pictures:
ARCHIV FÜR KUNST AND GESCHICHTE, London: pp.47, 57. ANCIENT ART & ARCHITECTURE COLLECTION, London: p.38. BRIDGEMAN ART LIBRARY, London: British Museum, London p.28; Private Collection p.1; Private Collection p.61; Private Collection p.63; Victoria & Albert Museum, London pp.6, 12–13, 15, 32, 36–37; Victor Lownes Collection, London p.42. E.T. ARCHIVE: Private Collection pp.9, 39, 41; Victoria & Albert Museum, London p.17. WERNER FORMAN ARCHIVE: India Office Library, London p.2; Philip Goldman Collection, London pp.21, 48; Private Collection pp.24, 26–27, 30, 43, 45, 51, 53, 55; Private Collection p.58.

Cover illustrations
Front: Tantric album painting, late 18th/19th century (WERNER FORMAN ARCHIVE/Private Collection)
Back: Lady and Prince Wrapped in Quilt (E.T. ARCHIVE/Victoria & Albert Museum)

CONTENTS

INTRODUCTION   IN WESTERN society sex has been used mostly for pleasure and procreation, while in Eastern cultures sex has a threefold purpose: pleasure, procreation, and as a means of expanding and exploring spirituality. In China this last use of sex is called *provoking the spirit*. This book is about how we in the West can provoke the spirit – how we can use sex not just as an expression of love but as a real way to make love and also as a technique of meditation and a path to enlightenment.

> *At the start of sexual union, keep watchful on the fire in the beginning and, so continuing, escape the embers at the end.*
>
> SHIVA

Religions in the East such as *Taoism* and *Tantric Buddhism* regard sex as one of the most natural activities that human beings can indulge in – they consider the only guilt to be if you debase or waste the sexual experience. What is natural can't be forbidden. What is joyful and harmonious can't be wrong. There can only be bliss and a path to awakening in the ecstasy of sexual fulfillment.

The sexual techniques and practices in this book have been drawn from a wide variety of ancient sexual texts including the Chinese *Tao of Sex* or *pillow books*, the Arabic *Perfumed Garden*, the Japanese *Shunga*, the Indian *Kama Sutra*, and the teachings of the *Tantric Buddhists*.

Feel free to change, adapt, try or leave out any of these techniques. They are the route to spiritual awareness through sex but they are not the final objective – that is up to you.

The Poem of the Pillow by Kitagawa Utamaro whose elegantly erotic work introduced Japanese ideas about sex and sexuality to the West.

1

THE
HARMONY
OF SEX

*The Taoist view
of orgasm.*

*How to make the
journey as pleasurable
as the arrival.*

IN CHINA the *Taoists* have always seen sex as a natural and pleasurable way to enrich and further their knowledge of the Universe. Even in the face of adversity and suffering the Taoists manage to maintain a serenity and acceptance. The same may be said of their sex life — *the one who knows the Tao sees but is not carried away by passion. Through the Tao a couple may be locked in lust but it is no earthly lust and that is why it brings such great good fortune.*

When we adopt the Taoist philosophy of that which is, is, then we can begin to let go of our expectations of 'sex'. The Taoists believe that the journey is as, if not more, important, than the destination. If we have expectations of our own or our partner's response during sex we will be unsatisfied — if we accept that whatever is happening is perfect then we can only find satisfaction. The Taoists place less emphasis on orgasm because of this. For them not all sex has to end in orgasm — sometimes the journey can be so pleasurable that an orgasm would detract from this pleasure. In the West we are relentlessly goal-orientated, especially in our sex life — for us sex without orgasm would seem unnatural. However, our sex experience can often seem unsatisfactory exactly because of this inability to enjoy the journey of sex without constantly projecting ahead to the future orgasm. We, in the West, talk about *achieving* an orgasm or a *climax* as if it were the only objective in sex.

In the Taoist tradition, sexual union is a long, slow, pleasurable journey with much to see and enjoy along the way, not a heated rush to climax.

During the journey of sex the Chinese place a strong emphasis on sensual kissing, which they regard as so erotic and private that they rarely kiss passionately in public.

EXERCISE
SENSUAL KISSING

In the harmony of yang and yin (see page 18) the tongue is considered male, the penis, while the lips are considered female, the vulva. Thus we each have elements of the other's sex.

Your mouth should be relaxed and happy.

Sensual kissing can be enjoyed whenever a couple wish. They may be too tired for sex but kissing requires much less energy. Always use sensual kissing as a preliminary to sex and especially during and afterward.

Clean teeth and fresh breath make for more harmonious kissing so be careful with your oral hygiene. The Chinese, especially in medicine, regard the tongue as the only internal organ that is externally visible. It is a very sensitive organ and, used sensually, can be capable of extreme pleasure. You can use your tongue to explore your partner's lips, mouth, teeth and tongue. You can nip their lips very softly with your teeth, suck their tongue and even exchange saliva – this is called *jade fluid*. If for health or hygiene reasons you prefer not to do this you can leave it out. If it's a question of your feeling hesitant then maybe you don't feel as passionately about your partner as you think you do – tasting your partner's jade fluid requires love and trust.

Sensual kissing shouldn't be restricted to your partner's mouth alone. You can use your lips and tongue to explore every part of his or her own body while your partner explores yours. If you start with the mouth you can move on to kissing the entire face – eyelids and ears are especially sensitive.

Be aware of your other senses as well, especially of smell. As your partner becomes aroused the body scent will change. By learning these subtle variations of aroma you can become a better lover – not moving on until you have detected the smell of arousal, or speeding up once you have.

While you are kissing your partner's mouth and face you can use your hands to caress his or her face as well. You can use your fingers as well as your tongue – exploring the lips with your finger tips while your tongue caresses your partners. The only rule with sensual kissing is to take your time – as there is no orgasm goal you can carry on as long as you both like, although if it is sensual enough either of you may orgasm through the pleasure of kissing alone. Some women find sensual kissing so pleasurable that they quite often spontaneously have an orgasm.

Learn to listen while you are kissing – each tiny sound your partner makes means something. By learning what each of these sounds mean you can learn how your partner's body responds and thus move more in tune with your partner. Take your time to use all your senses to explore every part of your partner's body.

LEFT *A slow, languorous exploration of each other's face and body, using hands and mouths, fingers and tongues, is a pleasurable way to learn how to respond to the tiny shifts and changes in your partner's state of arousal.*

OVER PAGE *Sensual kissing brings intimacy and swooning pleasure to sex. Even if it is not a prelude to penetrative sex it can provide a delicious low-energy interval of affectionate harmony. Male and female have equal powers, and yin and yang are perfectly balanced when sensual kissing is done with thought and consideration.*

2

SECURITY
AND CARING

*The importance
of touch.*

*How caressing can
unleash the flow of
ch'i energy.*

*Mutual caressing transmits
positive energy flow
between lovers.*

FOR THE CHINESE the Tao can be interpreted as *the way* that flows through everything. The way may be likened to a Western concept of God or spirit. If this energy or spirit flow moves through everything, then anything is a representation or container of God. Whatever we choose to worship thus contains the essence of God. The Taoists choose to place their emphasis on the human body as a focus for their spiritual attention. They regard the sex act as an act of supreme worship – and the daily buildup to sex such as kissing, touching and caressing as part of the ritual of worship.

The Taoists believe that by touching and caressing each other we stay in touch with ourselves – each caress given to another is a caress of ourselves. The more caressing we give, and thus get, the happier we become – the happier we become, the longer we live, the healthier we are, the more work we can do – the benefits are endless. As we caress each other energy flows in and through our bodies. The Taoists call this energy *ch'i*. Ch'i energy has a strength and vigor, certain directions it feels best flowing in, and receptive and positive qualities. The way the Taoists perceive ch'i energy flowing from body to body is that it is happiest when the man caresses his partner. A woman's ch'i is receptive and needs constant recharging from a man's more volatile ch'i or she is likely to grow dissatisfied and lethargic – likewise a man's "hot" ch'i needs to be constantly "earthed" to a woman's cooler ch'i or he will become restless and irritated.

EXERCISE
CARESSING

FOR THE MAN You need to be aware of the many changes that take place in your partner from first initial touching, through arousal, to orgasm. As you caress her body you should pay attention to her breathing: listen for any changes – does her breathing become shorter or deeper as she becomes more aroused? Some women's breath actually changes smell the closer to orgasm they get. Her overall aroma may change as well – smelling your partner is a very erotic act and it indicates a level of trust and respect that she will appreciate. Watch for changes in skin color and texture – her cheeks may flush redder, tiny beads of sweat may appear on her upper lip and forehead, her nipples harden. As her pleasure mounts she may make different sounds – by learning what each of these mean you can monitor her level of arousal and increase or reduce the level of caressing in a particular area.

Caressing can take the form of

Touching and stroking is a mutual activity. The man must be careful to arouse his partner's cool yin energy correctly while she must help him to contain his yang ardor until they are at the same level of arousal.

It is the responsibility of the male partner to excite and recharge the receptive but slow-moving female energy levels. Male energy is quickly aroused and needs the cooling languor of the female energy to prevent it from dissipating too quickly.

simply holding hands up to full massage or even sex itself. During sex your responsibility, according to the Tao, is to take charge – monitoring your partner's responses and adjusting your techniques accordingly. This is why the Tao places such emphasis on sex within a loving and secure relationship. How can sex get better or be used for spiritual advancement if you constantly have new partners? You need time to develop such a close rapport. Your role, as the male partner, is to control your own urge to achieve satisfaction until your partner has had her ch'i energy recharged fully.

FOR THE WOMAN If your partner's responsibility is to look after your needs first, then your role is to be as helpful to him as possible in order to enable him to be as good a lover as possible. The Tao explains that you should give your partner as much information as you can – tell him what feels right, what

arouses you and stop him from rushing too much – make him take each step slowly. You are dealing with complex energy issues here and they cannot be hurried. The interplay and exchange of ch'i energy takes time to be successful. You musn't excite your partner too

Touching, stroking and caressing should be a gentle, progressive activity just as intimate and affectionate when clothed as it is when you meet flesh to flesh.

quickly. The Tao recommends that you hold his *jade hammer* while he is caressing you (see page 22) but you should be cautious that he doesn't spill his *ching* too quickly. While he is caressing you, you are an embodiment of the Tao, the *Supreme Ultimate*, and, as such, a holy object – you are being worshipped. While you are being caressed you can monitor how the energy in your body feels. Close your eyes – what do you see? Listen to your inner voice – what does it tell you? Even in the states of the most intense arousal and orgasm you should keep a detachment so you can really appreciate how the energy flows within you.

FOR BOTH OF YOU Caressing can be just gentle touching with the hands or it can use every part of your body – stroking with the lips and tongue, using the breasts to caress the other's body, using your toes and feet, rubbing complete bodies together. The Tao says "stay in touch" – by doing so the ch'i energy flows making a complete circle of love.

3

YANG

AND YIN

THE CHINESE *TAOISTS* believe that the *Tao* is the harmonious balance of the Universe. From the Tao, *the Way*, comes everything. That everything can be divided into Heaven and Earth, matter and spirit, male and female. They call these two principles *Yang* and *Yin*.

Male and female energy explained.

How to make male and female energy complement each other.

Although the yang and yin are often seen as opposites they cannot exist without the other – within each there is always an element of the other – the tiny dot of white yang within the black yin, and the tiny dot of dark yin within the white of the yang.

The yang is the masculine principle; its properties are: *spirit, heaven, positive, active, male, creative, light, day, heat, hard, dry*. The yin is the feminine principle; its properties are *creation, earth, negative, passive, female, receptive, dark, night, cold, soft, wet*.

These differing properties of yin and yang give men and women a different approach to sexual experience and satisfaction.

The yang energy is much more immediate – hot and spontaneous. The yin energy is darker and cooler – taking longer to arouse, yet more prolonged and sustained. When we incorporate these principles into our lovemaking it becomes more satisfying because we are working with a real knowledge of how the energy differs. Together they form a perfect complement, without each other nothing is complete.

When we use the creative yang energy to stimulate the receptive yin energy it is a slower process than when we use the cool yin energy to stimulate the hot yang energy. We can look at some of these attributes in our partners. Does the man feel ready for sex more often in the morning in the light and heat of the day? And does the woman prefer the night – the cool and the dark? Does the woman take longer to become aroused but has deeper, more frequent orgasms? Is the man more stimulated by what he sees than the woman, who may prefer more emotional or subtle stimuli? Remember that there is no right or wrong with all of this – there just is.

EXERCISE
FEELING ENERGY

You need to do this one alternately over two days. The woman goes first (yin energy is slower to rise). Her partner washes and bathes her including shampooing her hair. He dries her all over. It might be useful to have a certain amount of warmth (an open fire?) and privacy for this exercise because it can take

quite a considerable time if you want to really enjoy it and learn the most from it. After drying her he can massage her body with essential oils (ylang-ylang, musk, patchouli, jasmine and sandalwood as preferred) taking great care to avoid the area around her vulva. The man should try to imagine his partner's body as a spiral with her vulva as the very center: the yin energy coiling its way inward. His massage should begin with the face, neck and shoulders before switching to the feet, calves and thighs. Next the arms, trunk and breasts and finally – the center of the spiral. The man should then (if she wants) give his partner an orgasm using his fingers, tongue and lips. Afterward he should hold his partner, keep caressing her, let her decide what she wants next – to sleep, to eat, whatever she herself decides.

On the next day or suitable occasion it is the woman's turn to give. She should bathe her

The Yin/Yang symbol clearly show how male and female energies come together to form a whole and how each contains a seed of the other deep within it.

partner, dry him and massage him using the essential oils he prefers. Her massage should again reflect the spiral but this time imagine the yang energy spiraling outward from his genitals, the center. The very first thing she should massage should be his penis – not to orgasm but as a caress – then his abdomen and thighs then, without letting go of his penis, continue with his chest, legs, arms, feet and face – all the while still holding his penis. This is important if the woman wants her man to feel secure and loved. Then (if he wants) the woman can bring him to orgasm using her hands, lips and mouth. Again afterward he also gets to choose exactly what he wants – to sleep if that's what he needs, and the woman should let him sleep still holding him, still caressing him.

You may find that the bathing and massaging are enough and you don't need an orgasm – remember: getting to know your

partner spiritually is what it is all about – feeling the energy shift and change as you massage or are massaged yourself. After you have both done this you may like to try doing it the other way around – does it feel different? Does the energy feel right? By learning how the energy flows we can make use of it in our love–making – we can also gain a wider knowledge of the Tao, yin and yang and spirituality.

Partners take it in turn to explore each other's energy patterns through sensitive touch and sensual massage. Such a dialog helps to find out what best raises the spirit in each other.

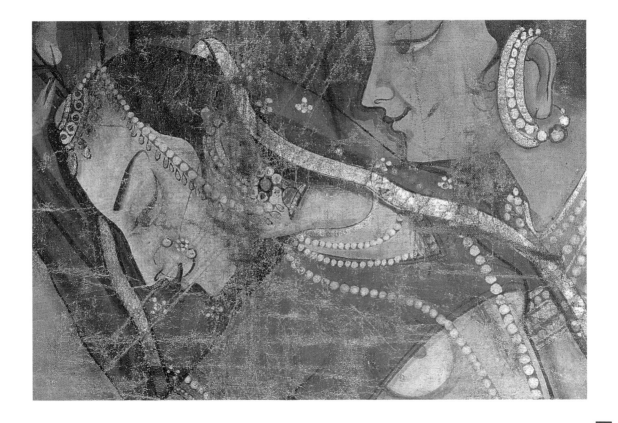

4

THE TAO
OF ENERGY

*The Tao energy
explained.*

*How to combine yin
and yang energies.*

THE TAOISTS BELIEVE that sex without love cannot contain any true ecstasy and that ecstasy is a combining not just of bodies but of souls as well. Souls are not made of matter but are constructed of pure energy. When we have sex with our partner we are accessing and exchanging that energy. We carry a residue of all the sexual energy we have ever exchanged with our previous sexual partners. If our partners have been loving then we will have incorporated some of that love into ourselves – but if the relationships were fraught and unhealthy we will carry that unhappiness. This is why the Tao places such emphasis on not changing partners too frequently; but the Tao also appreciates that when we are young the energy is strong and very active: we will need to experiment and explore to find out about our sexuality.

In the previous pages we looked at yin and yang. All the parts of the body are categorized according to that principle, as are the *dews and juices* of the body. Thus a man's *ching* or seminal fluid is yang, while a woman's vaginal secretions, *the stream of yin*, are yin. The man's penis, *yu heng*, is called the *jade hammer* or *jade stem* and is yang, and the woman's vulva, the *yu men*, is called the *jade gate* and is yin. The Tao is very concerned that the ch'i energy and the yin and yang are brought together in the correct combination.

In the Tao tradition, sexual union
provides the way for energy to flow
to and from each partner, bodies
and souls uniting in one ecstatic embrace.

The Tao has no place, unlike other esoteric sexual practices, for masturbation since it relies too predominantly on only yin or yang, but it does regard oral sex as a very good form of loving. For women cunnilingus is a recommended part of loving, while fellatio for a man is offered with some advice: basically it's to do with the spilling of ching too early. The younger a man is, then the more likely he is to be unable to retain control. Fellatio is recommended up to, but not beyond, the point of ejaculation. The Taoists consider that the vagina is the only proper recipient of ching – anywhere else and the energy flow is modified. However, there are many other esoteric sexual practices where the swallowing of semen is regarded as an essential part of the energy exchange. Perhaps you both would like to experiment – there is no right or wrong, only what *feels* right and that you can only find out by constant practice.

In the Tao tradition, oral sex is seen as a very effective way of making love and sharing energies. This advanced position is an Indian tantric pose; the same effect can be achieved in a less acrobatic manner, lying down in the traditional Western "69" pattern.

ORAL SEX ENERGY

Both partners adopt the "sixty-nine" position and enjoy oral sex alternately. The one being enjoyed talks about what can be felt with the eyes closed, what colors can be seen, where the energy is felt to be coming from. Then the one actually performing the oral sex stops and talks about what was felt, seen and sensed. Then it's the other's turn and again you talk about it. Continue this process up to and during orgasm. Take your time, there's no rush, and enjoy exploring how oral sex feels not only in your body but also in your spirit, and be aware of how the energy of oral sex feels coming from your partner when your partner is enjoying your doing it to him or her. **Follow up:** see how a greater knowledge of your partner's sexual energy can help you in other areas of your relationship. While a man may feel predominantly yang energy and the woman yin, there must always be the beginnings of the other within that energy, and there will always be times when the male will need to be in touch with his own yin energy and the woman with her yang energy – space must be given to allow this other energy to manifest, and its potential to be explored and given freedom to express itself.

EXERCISE
THE ENERGY OF ORGASM

For most of us in the West sex takes place predominantly "in our heads." This is where we go at the point of orgasm. Yet there is much to be gained from practicing the Tao way of staying in the present. You might like to try the following technique, which was recommended as long ago as 1500 B.C. Begin

with the man bringing his partner to orgasm either with his hands or during penetrative sex. He should monitor his partner's responses so he knows exactly when she is about to reach orgasm.

As she does so she should open her eyes and he should stare directly into them. This exercise should only be done if the partners are both deeply in love with each other because it requires a very deep level of trust and respect. As your partner reaches orgasm what can you see in her eyes? She might like to tell you afterward what she could feel. The partners should change around and the woman should bring her partner to orgasm and again stare deeply into his eyes just as he ejaculates. For both of you there may be an overwhelming desire to shut your eyes, to stay "in your mind." The other partner should then hold your face and gently remind you to "stay present" – even requesting you to "stay with me."

In tantric tradition, partners look deep into each other's eyes at the point of orgasm, staying together as they are rocked by the rush of kundalini energy.

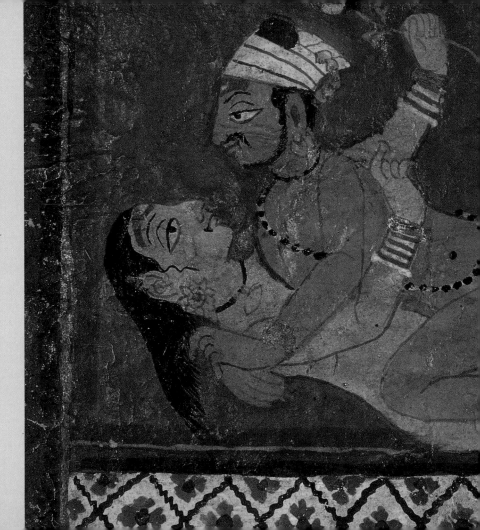

5
ORGASM AND SPIRITUALITY

For most of us in the West our orgasm marks the end of our sexual experience. Generally we reach our climax then hug each other, talk for a bit and, finally, go to sleep. That's it, we have had our sex and feel relaxed and loving.

Orgasm as a gateway to spirituality.

How to raise the kundalini energy through the chakras.

Tantric sex is based on a perfect union, with both partners committed to the same level of spiritual awareness.

But for the *tantric Buddhists* the orgasm is merely the beginning – the jumping off point for an intense religious and spiritual experience. For them the orgasm is solely a key to unlock a gateway to a richer and more fulfilling life: the orgasm is not just the physical release it is for us but a complex shifting of energy patterns up through the *chakras*.

These chakras are seven energy centers that are situated in our bodies, and tantric Buddhism is about

using sex to raise the *kundalini energy* from the *base chakra,* which is at the bottom of the spine, up through the centers to the *crown chakra,* which is situated on the top of the head. The kundalini energy is sometimes referred to as *serpent* or *sex* energy. It is supposed to be very powerful and, by raising it to the very top of the chakras, a person is freed from the cycle of life and death and rebirth. So we are dealing with sex here to free us from karma. Kundalini sex practices

THE SEVEN CHAKRAS

1 The Root or Base chakra

Situated just by the anus, it governs our instincts and primordial feelings and is the home of the kundalini energy.

2 The Sex chakra

Situated in the genitals, it governs our sex drive and need to procreate. During sex for most people this is as far up the chakra ladder as the kundalini energy will rise.

3 The Solar Plexus chakra

Situated in the pit of the stomach, it governs fear and our control over the outside world.

4 The Heart chakra

Situated over the heart, it governs our love.

5 The Throat chakra

Situated in the throat, it governs our ability to communicate.

6 The Brow chakra

Situated just behind our forehead (the third eye), it governs our intellect.

7 The Crown chakra

Situated on top of the head, it governs our spiritual life. It is said to be the home of Shiva and when the kundalini energy and the god Shiva are reunited then we are free, enlightened, released from the bounds of life and death.

place great emphasis on the perfect union of male and female – there's no point trying tantric practices without a partner who is on the same wavelength and has the same level of spiritual focus. The perfect state of union between the God Shiva and kundalini energy is called *moksha*, which is also the name which is given to a woman's orgasm.

For Westerners, learning how to raise kundalini energy once orgasm has been achieved requires practice, dedication and trust in your partner. To lovers who have been brought up in the tantric tradition it comes naturally.

EXERCISE

RAISING ENERGY

The tantric Buddhists emphasize how important orgasm is to unlocking the gateway to spirituality, so you both need to know how and when you best orgasm. You really need to orgasm simultaneously and that is probably best done with penetrative sex. Both of you need to keep your tongue touching the roof of your mouth. This completes the energy circuit and will allow the kundalini energy to flow back correctly. The tantras do talk of the energy getting stuck if this is not done.

FOR THE WOMAN As you reach orgasm you can tense and relax your vaginal muscles. Imagine your vulva as a pump – you are going to use the power of your orgasm and the lifting action of your vagina to pump the kundalini upward toward the crown chakra. By squeezing and releasing you will be able to

feel the energy rising up your spine. It may take the form of tingling like mild electricity and may be accompanied by a feeling of warmth spreading out along your limbs to tingle at your fingertips and toes.

FOR THE MAN As you reach orgasm you can use the muscles in your buttocks to pump the kundalini energy upward. You may feel it rising up your spine as if it were a column of cool water – quite different from the sensations your partner feels.

FOR BOTH OF YOU After you have reached orgasm keep the pumping action going (and your tongue touching the roof of your mouth) for as long as you can. When you can do no more, allow your body to relax slowly – letting the kundalini energy drain back into the root chakra where it belongs. In the tantric tradition, raising kundalini energy is a lifetime dedication and a spiritual focus of intense devotion to Shiva.

According to Taoist tradition, sex should be relaxed, leisurely and enjoyable for both parties. The aim is to mingle and enhance each other's spiritual energy, not for one partner to dominate the other physically or mentally.

THE *HUANG-TI NEI CHING SU WEN* (the Yellow Emperor's classic of Internal Medicine) dating back to the Shang dynasty (1523-1028 B.C.) contained the first Taoist sex techniques. In it Huang Ti, the Yellow Emperor, asks questions of his adviser, Qi Po, and is given answers. Qi Po tells him that when a couple practice sex correctly they will stay young and healthy, increase in strength and vigor and live longer – but if they squander their sex they will suffer ill health and premature aging.

6
....
THE MALE ORGASM

The male orgasm explained in Taoist terms.

How to control ejaculation and prolong orgasm.

This squandering was regarded as the lack of enjoying the journey. Couples were advised that if they wanted to benefit from the Tao they had to learn how to breathe long and deeply, have a sense of security, have agreement of will so there would be no opposition in their love-making, eat neither too much nor too little beforehand or during, make sure the temperature was pleasant and, finally, relax and enjoy sex – and that the best sex would be when the woman was completely satisfied when it was over but that the man would not yet be exhausted.

Basically the female orgasm was deemed very important while the male ejaculation was seen as

The male orgasm should be postponed for as long as possible so that female orgasm energy can reach full flow.

secondary. In this lies the most fundamental difference between East and West love techniques – for the Tao says that the male ejaculation is separate from his orgasm. In the West the two happen simultaneously and we come to believe they are the same thing – in the East the ejaculation is seen to be for procreation, and retained as much as possible, while the male orgasm can be indulged in as much as the man likes or needs. A lot of confusion has resulted from this Taoist *retaining of seed* and some practitioners of Taoist love techniques have become confused. It is this separation of orgasm from ejaculation that is so important. Nowhere in the Tao does it say that the man shouldn't have orgasms – only that he should retain his seed wherever possible. The tantric Buddhists agree on this point and recommend the retaining of ejaculation as a prerequisite to raising the kundalini energy.

EXERCISE

CONTROLLING

EJACULATION

Once it becomes clear in your mind that ejaculation and male orgasm are *not* the same thing these exercises will become easier.

The first thing you have to do is know your sexual rhythms quite well. Only you know how quickly or how slowly you reach orgasm and which positions are better or worse for you. Assuming you are having penetrative sex, and you will need your partner's full support and understanding for this, when you first feel you are reaching the point of orgasm raise your waist so that your penis is lodged hard against your partner's vaginal wall. You can withdraw your penis an inch or so, so that you lock or stop the orgasm. When you feel your orgasm subside you can continue thrusting. Again stop and lock whenever you feel you are entering the first stages of orgasm. It is important to stop before you feel that the orgasm is coming on too strongly.

The second method of stopping your ejaculation is to squeeze hard with your forefinger and thumb a point midway between your scrotum and anus. This works best if your partner is on top in which case she can do it for you. The squeeze method will also probably make you lose your erection, but when you reinsert your soft penis you should have no problem getting it erect again. As the Tao says: *the good lover can enter soft and exit hard.*

If you follow the principle of nine shallow thrusts to one deep thrust and then rest for a moment, you should be able, using either the lock or squeeze method, to have penetrative sex almost without stopping. If you find nine thrusts too exciting start off with three and build up through six to nine.

The reason a lot of women in the West can bring about orgasm only through clitoral stimulation is that most men are unable to have penetrative sex for very long. By not having an ejaculatory orgasm you can keep going for much longer and thus satisfy your partner much better. Once you have practiced non-ejaculatory sex for a while you will find that you can reach orgasm without loss of semen. This Taoist practice takes time. The orgasm you have will be much more intense than normal and is called the *Plateau of Delight,* while an ejaculatory orgasm is a *Peak of Ching.* The plateau suggests you can keep going higher, which is true. The idea of a man having multiple orgasms is new in the West but quite possible – and all without loss of semen.

BACKGROUND: *Women can help their partners learn to control ejaculation by stimulating an erection and then holding it, using the squeeze method described above.*

OVER PAGE *Separating orgasm from ejaculation is an important technique in both Taoist and tantric traditions. It allows the man to match his timing with his partner and to experience multiple orgasms without energy-sapping ejaculation.*

7

THE FEMALE ORGASM

The female orgasm explained in Taoist terms.

How to explore the quality of female energy through masturbation.

MOST OF THE ancient sexual texts agree that women don't lose energy through their orgasm: rather that they take in or absorb the male energy. Releasing the kundalini energy at the point of orgasm is usually much easier for women than it is for men because of this retaining of their own energy as well as receiving the man's. And because there is little or no energy loss, masturbation, for women, is regarded as much more beneficial than it is for men. The visual art of the Orient pictures women enjoying self-love much more often than men because of the difference in energy flow.

Only you, a woman, can know and explore your own body to such an intimate degree that you can generate your own orgasms to order. The knowledge thus gained can be used to guide and instruct your partner to enable him to bring you to orgasm just as easily as you can yourself. Part of being in an

Male partners should learn how their female lovers like to be touched to achieve ecstatic orgasm.

honest and loving relationship is being able to express what you need and want without inhibition. By exploring your own body you become an expert – a teacher.

EXERCISE
FEMALE SPIRITUAL
ORGASM

You need to do this exercise over several days so that you can compare before and after. First bring yourself to orgasm as you would do normally and be aware afterward how you feel: is there any guilt? Sometimes we feel very liberated but carry a residue of our Western upbringing. Are you more relaxed? Do you feel satisfied or merely temporarily sated? The next day (or later on the same day if you want) bring yourself to orgasm again but this time keep your tongue touching the roof of your mouth to complete the energy circle. You should also concentrate on your third eye (the

For women, masturbation is in itself a spiritual act because it raises the kundalini energy in homage to the divine. Women exploring their own bodies so that they can teach their partners to be more receptive is also in accordance with the Taoist principles, because female energy is not dissipated in the orgasms created by masturbation.

space between your eyes and slightly above and into your forehead). As you reach orgasm tightly squeeze your vaginal muscles and imagine your vulva as a pump. It is going to push the energy up your spine, through the chakras, to the top of your head. You will be carrying out an act of intense spirituality – not just mere masturbation – a devotion and offering to Shiva. There are several different types of orgasm for women. Perhaps you would like to explore those which, if not all, you prefer.

THE CLITORAL ORGASM The Chinese refer to the clitoris as the *pearl on the jade step* and a woman's orgasm as *bursting of the clouds,* which is certainly a lot more imaginative and helpful than some of our Western terms. The clitoris swells, becomes engorged and enlarged with blood when stimulated and can be found quite easily. It can be caressed with fingers, and by your partner's

tongue and lips as well as stroked, licked, sucked and blown on with soft breath. Some women can hardly bear having their clitoris touched because it is so sensitive, other women can tolerate quite considerable force being applied to it – every woman is different. Most women, however, find that it is unbearably sensitive immediately after orgasm. A useful technique to alleviate this is the *panting breath orgasm*. Up to and during orgasm you pant vigorously: keep your tongue slightly extended and pant from your belly rather than from your mouth. Again you need an understanding partner if you are not doing this alone. The clitoral sensitivity usually disappears if you try this – it also helps bring on your orgasm more quickly if you are nearly there, but if you are not then it can help you delay your orgasm if you want.

VAGINAL ORGASM Some women find this quite hard to effect owing sometimes to

One useful technique for female orgasm is for the woman to stimulate herself while her partner concentrates on controlling his ejaculation. When she is ready, they can join in deep penetrative sex and enjoy simultaneous orgasms.

their partner being too quick or not sensitive enough. Your partner may need a little time to learn ejaculation control – when he has he will be able to thrust deeper and longer, which may well help you effect vaginal orgasm. Another technique is to stimulate your clitoris until you are about to orgasm and then switch to deep penetrative sex at the last moment and effect orgasm that way (this doesn't work for all women). The ancient texts approved of the use of the *harigata* (Japan) or *lingam* (India) as a penis substitute used either alone by the woman or, as an aid to intercourse, by the man. Many modern equivalents are available and can be helpful while your partner is still learning how to control and regulate his own ejaculation.

G-SPOT ORGASM Most women (but not all) have an extremely sensitive area on the vagina's front wall about half to two-thirds of the way in. During penetrative sex (the man kneeling, you lying backward with your feet crossed on his chest) your partner should be able to stimulate the G-spot with his fingers, as well as stimulating your clitoris and, using his penis, also stimulate your vaginal walls. It may be possible, with practice, to have all three types of orgasm simultaneously.

This tantric pose is a very effective way to find the elusive G-spot.

8

SEX AS A
MEDITATION

*Tantric sex as a
way to God.*

*How to use sex for
divine meditation.*

TANTRIC SEX IS used as a means of getting in touch with God. Western traditions don't seem to include sexual activity as a means of doing this. However, it has long been a part of Eastern practice to use sex not only for pleasure but also to dedicate the time spent during sex to a higher focus.

EXERCISE

TWO AS ONE

MEDITATION

This sex meditation is one of the oldest and most widely used tantric practices. The man should sit with his legs outstretched. His partner should sit astride him, with his penis inserted into her vulva. She can then wrap her legs around his back and he should bring his legs up under her buttocks. His hands should rest lightly on her shoulders and hers on his forearms. This is the classic *lotus sex* position. You, as a couple, should now gently look into each other's eyes. If you are both used to

Sex as a meditative process, where partners are motionless yet intimately linked is underrated in the West, where athletic thrusting is often considered the only way to ecstasy.

A variation on the lotus sex position. Maintaining eye contact and inwardly focusing on your partner's chakras transforms sex into an act of profound meditation.

meditating, this position can be held for quite some time without discomfort. If meditation is new to you then you may need to help support yourselves with cushions or practice for only short periods to begin with until you become comfortable with the position.

Your concentration, while in the lotus sex position, should start with the base chakra (see page 29) of your partner and you should try to feel warmth and energy radiating from that area. Slowly move the feeling upward through the chakras. By maintaining eye contact at all times you should be able to know exactly what your partner is feeling.

As the feeling is moved upward you may feel yourself growing closer to orgasm. There is no need to move to encourage this. The lotus sex position should enable you both to orgasm without any effort. Like everything, it takes practice and, with or without orgasm, it is valuable time spent meditating and being extremely close with your partner.

Western interest in the liberating Eastern view of sex as a positive, natural and spiritually empowering activity is not new. This charming 18th-century book illustration shows a couple of young European lovers attempting a version of the lotus sex position.

9

THE CONSCIOUSNESS OF SEX

Sex as a conscious act.

How to anchor yourself in the Tao "here and now".

IF YOU FOUND the position in the previous exercise somewhat uncomfortable you can try this: the man sits on a chair (one with no arms) with his knees together and his partner sits astride him; his erect penis should be inserted into her vulva.

You can both now visualize an energy circuit that begins in your base chakras, runs up your spines and combines at the top of your heads. You can look into each other's eyes and even practice sensual kissing (see pages 10 and 11). By locking your tongues together you will complete the energy circle. Stay like this for a while and feel what happens to the energy within your bodies.

The sensations and experiences of sex can be so intense and acute that they can be used to anchor you into the present – the *here and now* of the Tao. By concentrating on the feelings within you spiritually rather than

In the Tibetan Buddhist tradition, the consciousness of the power of sex is recognized in Vajravahari, a Dakini, or demon goddess, the personification of intense passion.

physically you may experience heightened perception and an increased awareness of that energy that keeps you alive.

EXERCISE
STAYING PRESENT

In an earlier exercise we experimented with looking into each other's eyes just at the point of orgasm.

You can take this further: at the point of orgasm again look into your partner's eyes and say aloud whatever it is you want to, such as "I love you." And when you say this be aware the "you" that you are loving is a universal you – you are loving the "you" in your partner, which is the same "you" that is in yourself. As you orgasm together you should feel the connection between us all – the energy that flows from one to another. By staying present at the point of orgasm you can feel this energy so much more strongly.

After orgasm, as you sink into that afterglow, you can close your eyes and meditate by concentrating on your third eye. Sometimes it's good to have a code worked out with your partner, for example a simple hand squeeze that means you wish to be alone with the universe for a moment and your partner shouldn't speak or move for a while.

After orgasm, you can continue your meditation by closing your eyes and concentrating on the inner universe.

49

The orgasm has been described as a lightning flash that, for a merest moment, illuminates the hidden face of God. Maybe this is why we seek it so often. By staying present during orgasm you will find your orgasms become longer and are more easily maintained, grow deeper and more intense – the flashes become searchlights for a while.

Any meditation techniques that you are used to practicing can be utilized for sex – chanting, visualizations, affirmations, breathing techniques, Zen – whatever you want to try. Obviously you need the support of your partner in any of this.

EXERCISE
STANDING PRESENT

Again an old tantric technique for staying in the here and now. You both stand up having penetrative sex. The woman should lock one leg around her partner's legs to help you both maintain balance. Both of you should place your right hand on the top of the other's head and your left hand held firmly against the small of the other's back. Again you can practice sensual kissing or maintain eye contact. This time feel the energy being drawn up from your feet, up your legs, up your spine and into your head. You may be able to feel when the energy reaches the top of your partner's head by a sudden flooding of warmth there.

You can move in this position if you want to, to bring each other to orgasm.

EXERCISE
PERINEUM
MEDITATION

Both partners adopt the "sixty-nine" position but instead of practicing oral sex each places the tongue on the other's *perineum* – the place midway between the anal opening and the scrotum in men and the vaginal opening in women. The perineum is extremely sensitive and the home of the root chakra. This is where the kundalini energy is when it is at rest; it is usually aroused during sex so this perineum meditation should be practiced without either partner being particularly aroused beforehand.

Once you have your tongue on your partner's perineum you will be able to feel the energy begin to move. Merely adopting this position is arousing and quite erotic. The energy should move fairly quickly and you may be surprised how strongly you can feel the kundalini serpent uncoil and begin to move. By just tongue pressure it may be possible to bring each other to orgasm – but it isn't essential – this is an exercise to feel the energy and to complete the circle of energy from a different angle. Does it feel different?

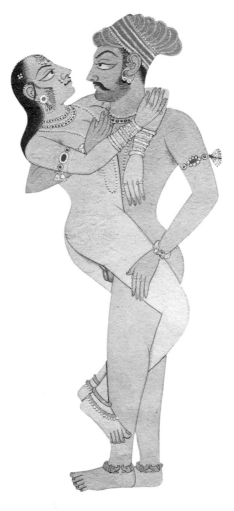

An ancient tantric position for remaining in the here and now during sex. This standing position offers a straight upward path for the kundalini energy, which gushes up from the base chakra and can be felt at the crown chakra, on the top of the head.

10

THE POSITIONS OF SACRED SEX

Traditional Eastern sex manuals.

How to achieve classic sexual positions.

THE INDIAN *Kama Sutra* and its companion texts the *Ananga Ranga* and the *Perfumed Garden* are probably the world's best-known but least-read sex manuals. Most people will have heard of them but never have seen a copy. The *Kama Sutra* was written sometime around A.D. 300, the *Ananga Ranga* around A.D. 1150 and the *Perfumed Garden* around A.D. 1600. All three were first translated into English by Sir Richard Burton just over a hundred years ago. They are manuals not just of sex positions but of advice on health, sex manners, hygiene, cultivation of the five senses, yoga and successful relationships.

Man on top is still the most favored position for many Western lovers.

They were written to bring together a union of body with spirit. They recommended a total equality between men and women with each being capable of, and requiring, good regular sexual experiences to be whole and complete human beings. Nowhere do these three texts consider sex immoral. Sex, for the early Hindus, was an open, exciting and spiritually uplifting experience. They urged experimentation and variety, getting to know each other's bodies intimately, and most of all, pleasure and enjoyment from sex.

There are only about three basic sex positions mentioned in the *Kama Sutra* – the rest are variations. The three are as follows

MAN ON TOP This includes the *Yawning Position*, where the man is on top with his partner's legs open fairly wide. It is close to the Western "missionary" position. The *Kama Sutra* describes various modifications to this including the *Clasping Position* where the woman's legs are wrapped around her partner's back, the *Pressing Position* where both partner's keep their legs straight and one presses the legs firmly along the outside of the other's, the *Crab Position* where the woman pulls her knees up against her stomach, the *Position of the Wife of Indra* where the woman pulls her knees tightly up to her chest, and the *Turning Position* where the man lies facing his partner's feet.

WOMAN ON TOP This includes the *Swing Position* where the woman, being on

In the Kama Sutra, there are many variations given to the man-on-top basic theme. This is a version of the Clasping Position, which allows for deep penetration.

top and facing her partner's feet, clasps his ankles and swings herself backward and forward, and the *Pair of Tongs Position* where the woman sits astride her partner facing his head with her knees bent either side of him.

MAN BEHIND This includes the *Congress of a Cow Position* where the man stands behind his partner and enters her from behind while she bends forward and touches the floor with her hands, and the *Elephant Position* where the man enters the woman from behind while she is lying face down.

The *Kama Sutra* says that you can use your imagination and copy any animal positions that you want to.

The *Ananga Ranga* describes many more positions but again they are mostly variations on the three basic ones of the *Kama Sutra*. The *Ananga Ranga* does give the lotus sex position practiced by the tantric Buddhists (see page 44) as well as an interesting variation: the *Cupped Position*. Here you both lie on your sides facing each other with your legs straight. The man enters from the front and friction for orgasm is generated by both partners bending and unbending their knees in turn. Without orgasm, it can be used as another meditation position.

The *Perfumed Garden* lists some eleven positions, most of which we have covered; a couple of interesting additions are:

THE FROG POSITION Here the man sits with his knees bent but pushed outwards. His partner lies with her knees drawn up tight against his chest. He grips her shoulders and pulls her slightly upright and she grips her own calves. Penetration cannot be very deep in this position but it is found to be an extremely intimate and relaxing position.

THE TAIL OF THE OSTRICH Here the woman lies on her back and the man kneels between her legs. He inserts his penis and his partner raises her legs until her heels are resting on his shoulders. She can arch her back until only her head and shoulders are still in contact with the bed (or ground or whatever). Her partner should grip her legs and can lower or raise her to achieve deep penetration or stimulation.

In the traditional Eastern books devoted to sexual techniques and manners, lovers are encouraged to try out as many different positions as feel comfortable. Learning new positions helps to focus the mind on the sexual act.

11

ATTITUDES
TO SEX

The poverty of Western sex revealed.

How to love yourself and help your partner to love you.

Touching and caressing each other throughout the day, before you go to bed, will always heighten the pleasure and profundity of your sexual acts.

SEX IS A VERY intimate act and when we practice spiritual sex it becomes even more so – we are opening not only our bodies but our souls as well. Any disagreements during the day will only affect us in bed later – good sex comes from a good relationship. If you haven't spent time touching and caressing prior to going to bed together there will be no strong bond or connection – there may be sex and it may, by Western standards, be good sex but it won't go beyond a fulfillment of bodily needs.

After you have practiced spiritual sex for a while you may well find that returning to your old sexual habits is profoundly disappointing – the old satisfaction will have proved itself to be shallow and unrewarding compared with your newfound sense of depth and intensity of experience.

Because we live in a Western society we continually pick up conscious and unconscious messages that sex is a sin, that it is in some way dirty, that we shouldn't enjoy it quite so much and that we shouldn't explore our own bodies. These messages are part of our negative programming and we have to work quite hard to replace them with thoughts that are more positive and life-affirming.

EXERCISE
LOOKING

AND LOVING

Try to start each day by looking at yourself naked in a full-length mirror and really appreciating what you see – this is what your partner, your lover, sees. Don't stand there criticizing – that's just more negative programming. Tell yourself you're fabulous, that you love yourself. Be turned on by what you see – it turns your lover on – then appreciate all that you can now see. You can use your hands to explore your body – feel the smoothness of your skin – it's a fabulous container of all that is you.

You can also do this exercise with your partner. Look at each other – see what your partner sees. You both may not feel exactly happy with your bodies, their shape or size. Reassure each other that you love each other just as you are. You can caress each other,

arouse each other, feel and see what your partner sees and feels in you. You can also laugh at each other, gently, in fun. Sex is a funny affair sometimes and the ability to laugh is one of the most treasured gifts. If you learn to laugh with each other during this exercise it becomes easier to laugh with each other when you're having sex together. We all have moments when something goes wrong – we get cramp or can't get an erection, our bodies make sudden unexpected noises – then the ability to laugh rather than be embarrassed is all-important. If you and your partner are really close then you will understand in those moments. How can you build such rapport together if you don't practice occasionally?

Nurturing intimacy and affection, learning to trust each other in play makes it easier to abandon restraint and entrust your partner with your soul's secrets when you are embraced in the ecstasy of spiritual sex.

57

EXERCISE
T A K I N G   T I M E

Most of the Indian sexual texts such as the *Kama Sutra* don't see sex as a separate activity from the rest of life as we tend to in the West – they were all for enjoying and indulging the other senses at the same time. Try taking some of your favorite foods to bed with you. These can be eaten, not as a separate activity, but while you are still locked in a passionate embrace. You can keep the fun and laughter going by eating messy foods such as fruit yogurt while enjoying sex.

Play your favorite music together – try different types of music and see how each affects the energy levels you both feel. Adopt the lotus sex position and just listen to the music. Take time to enjoy being with each other very closely and being at one with the universe together.

Wherever you make love create different atmospheres – light candles, perfume the room, enhance the textures of the bed covers (making love on silk is very different from making love on nylon!), change where and how you make love – outdoors, different rooms, different places, different times of day, different moods. This isn't just about "pepping up" your sex life by making it a bit spicy – it's about getting rid of all the old conditioning so you can be free to express sexually whatever you want – you can't be free if you have inhibitions or reserve, you can't take time if you feel goal-orientated to orgasm, you can't begin to find yourself spiritually while you hold on to your concepts about what should or shouldn't happen during sex. Expect nothing and you can be filled – expect something and you are already too full to receive anything. Esoteric sex literature placed great emphasis on the preparations needed for good sex.

Combining the sensual pleasures of food and sex can make a delicious time. Aim to include all the senses – smell, touch, taste, sound and sight – for a truly celebratory sexual experience.

12

THE SPIRITUALITY OF THE EROTIC

Japanese sexual traditions.

How to dress for erotic effect.

THE JAPANESE HAVE always had a healthy and liberal approach to good sex. Japanese brides were sent off to their weddings with a copy of a sex manual of explicit pictures so that, despite being virgins, they would know what to do and be prepared for a full and enjoyable sex life. These sex manuals are called *shunga,* which means *spring pictures.* They are full of pictures and drawings of couples in the most explicit action which, by Western standards, would be considered pornographic: the Japanese see them, however, as educational as well as arousing.

The couples in the shunga are usually depicted with exaggerated genitals. This is to focus attention on them so that the reader can see exactly what is going on – which bits go where. The couples are also very rarely shown naked: there is no element of prudishness intended in this but rather it stems from an awareness of how a partially undressed lover can be more erotic than one who is completely nude.

There is no area of human sexual activity that is missing from the shunga – masturbation, sex aids, lesbianism, aphrodisiacs, fantasies and nearly fifty different positions are included but always the emphasis is on the erotic and exciting nature of sex.

The shunga are based on the traditions passed down from the old religion of Japan, *Shinto*, which advocates sex as a natural and pleasing way to enhance spirituality.

EXERCISE

DRESSING FOR

YOUR LOVER

The shunga express the erotic nature of partially dressed sex so as to be sexually

stimulating. We can try the same approach. Dressing sexually and provocatively for your partner is often frowned upon in the West where sex is not supposed to be enjoyed. However good sex, and sex leading to a rewarding spiritual life, has to be liberated

An illustration from a Japanese shunga, a sex manual that was at once instructive and erotic.

and open. There is nothing wrong with dressing for your lover. Try making love without removing too much clothing. The friction of fabrics and unusual materials can be exciting and different. Experiment with your sexual attitudes – try wearing each other's clothing to see how it feels to be each other. The only drawback to dressing for your lover is when it becomes a fetish and your partner can't become aroused unless you wear a certain item or can only reach sexual satisfaction by doing a certain thing.

EXERCISE
SEDUCTIVE SEX

Seduction is a very exciting and important part of sex. It plays a significant role at the beginning of a relationship but can get lost along the way. Plan and prepare an evening when you will again seduce your partner –

prepare yourself in advance to wear what your partner likes, cook his or her favorite foods, prepare the bedroom (or wherever) with candles and incense, have the right music ready. Sometimes it can be interesting to satisfy your partner sexually without you too being sexually attended to. This form of dedication is one of total giving. Try it on alternate nights (or days) and see how it feels to give and then receive.

EXERCISE
HANDS AND LIPS

The shunga place great store by mutual masturbation and oral sex as methods of enjoying sexual experience while focusing on a spiritual encounter. Whoever is the recipient can lie back, enjoy the sensations and concentrate on his or her inner feelings and energies – without having to *do* anything. The shunga calls mutual masturbation the *hands that speak*. You can bring your partner to orgasm using your hands and lips, tongue and caresses, as a perfect gift of love. Your partner can repay the gift later but there should be no pressure to do so – a gift is a gift.

EXERCISE
FOREPLAY AND SEX

The Taoists refer to the *inner elixir* as the state when the fluids and secretions necessary to good sex are flowing and harmonious. If penetrative sex takes place before a woman's vaginal secretions are flowing and moist it is painful for both her and her partner. In the West foreplay is seen as a forerunner to intercourse while in the East it is seen as a complete and whole part of the sexual experience in itself. Foreplay doesn't have to end with intercourse – it can be a way of

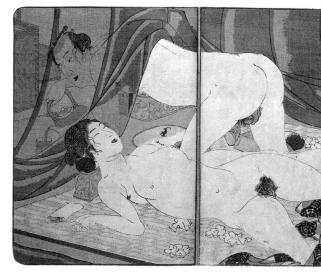

stimulating and encouraging a good sexual response. If a partner suffers from impotence, premature ejaculation, or is sexually unresponsive, then foreplay can be a useful method of relieving the pressure of having to have penetrative sex.

According to tantric and Taoist thought, sex that is fully satisfying both spiritually and physically should leave the woman replete but not exhaust the male partner.

INDEX